THE WORLD'S 60 BEST BRUNCH DISHES... PERIOD.
VÉRONIQUE PARADIS

PHOTOGRAPHER: Antoine Sicotte
ART DIRECTORS: Antoine Sicotte & Véronique Paradis
GRAPHIC DESIGNER: Laurie Auger
COVER DESIGNER: Laurie Auger
FOOD STYLIST: Véronique Paradis
ENGLISH TRANSLATOR: Lorien Jones
COPY EDITOR: Anna Phelan

PROJECT EDITOR: Antoine Ross Trempe

ISBN: 978-2-920943-48-3

Legal Deposit: 2013
Bibliothèque et Archives du Québec
Library and Archives Canada
ISBN: 978-2-920943-48-3

The publisher acknowledges the financial support of the Government of Canada through the Canada Book Fund (CBF) for its publishing activities and the support of the Government of Quebec through the tax credits for book publishing program (SODEC).

Originally published under the title
"Les 60 meilleurs brunchs du monde... Point final."

PRINTED IN CANADA

 Discover our upcoming books and much more!
WWW.FACEBOOK.COM/THEWORLDS60BEST

THE WORLD'S 60 BEST

BRUNCH DISHES

PERIOD.

THE WORLD'S 60 BEST

BRUNCH DISHES

PERIOD.

ABOUT THIS BOOK

The 60 brunch dishes in this book are, *in our opinion*, the 60 best brunch dishes in the world. Our team of chefs, writers, and foodies explored everything the culinary world has to offer to create this collection of the world's 60 best brunch dishes.

We based our recipes on the following criteria:

QUALITY OF INGREDIENTS
ORIGINALITY
TASTE
APPEARANCE
SIMPLICITY

Are these our personal favorite brunch dishes? Of course! But rest assured, our team of passionate, dedicated gourmets put time and loving care into formulating and testing each recipe in order to provide you with the 60 best brunch dishes ever. In fact, our chef brought each freshly made dish straight from the kitchen into the studio—no colorants, no sprays, no special effects added—and after each photo shoot, our creative team happily devoured the very brunch dishes you see in these photos.

We hope you'll enjoy discovering these recipes and using this book as much as we enjoyed making it.

TABLE OF CONTENTS

INTRO

Every one of the 60 best brunch dishes in this book features a flavor and cost legend (see pages 018 and 019) to guide your taste buds as well as your wallet in choosing the perfect dish. You will also find a glossary of culinary terms (page 029), handy cooking tips and tricks (page 025), and a list of must-have kitchen tools (page 023) that will help you create the world's BEST brunch dishes. Finally, use the easy-to-follow table of contents (pages 010 and 011) and ingredients index (pages 176 to 179) to find everything you're looking for.

Impress guests with your food knowledge from our informative "Did you know?" sidebars, and take your meals to the next level thanks to our tasty tips and serving suggestions!

Bon appétit!

TIME

SWEET

RICH

COST

LEGEND

 PREPARATION TIME IN MINUTES, INCLUDING COOKING TIME

SWEET • FRUITY

 LOW   MEDIUM   HIGH

CREAMY • BUTTERY • LUSCIOUS

 LOW   MEDIUM    HIGH

COST OF INGREDIENTS

 LOW   MEDIUM   HIGH

A SHORT HISTORY OF BRUNCH

The word brunch is a combination of the words *breakfast* and *lunch*. It's obvious what the word means, but historians aren't sure exactly how it was coined: some date it back to an article written in Britain in 1895, proposing that brunch would be the ideal first meal of the day after a rather boisterous night out (essentially, a hangover remedy), while others credit it to New York Morning Sun reporter Frank Ward O'Malley, on the newspaper's staff from 1906 until 1919, who used the word to describe the typically frazzled newspaper reporter's penchant for putting off breakfast until midday. In America, brunch fever gripped the nation after the end of World War I when church attendance dropped, which opened up time for long, leisurely Sunday meals.

Brunch is typically served midday, between 11 a.m. and 3 p.m., combines both the sweet and savory elements of breakfast and lunch dishes, and is served buffet-style or *à la carte*. Traditionally a popular way to celebrate Easter and Mother's Day, brunch is now a weekend ritual for many, from young families to bleary-eyed folks who normally wouldn't bother waiting for a table, but on weekends stand outside the hip brunch spot *du jour* in the hopes of a hearty meal (and maybe a mimosa or two) to help recover from last night's revelry.

But what it really comes down to is the food! Hotels often serve "continental breakfast," a light (and usually pretty dismal) complimentary meal of pastries, juice, tea, and coffee. A classic "English breakfast" is a more lavish affair, and includes eggs, potatoes, baked beans, mushrooms and tomatoes, fried bread, and black or white pudding. Scandinavian brunches consist of a variety of cold dishes, like smoked salmon with dill and cream cheese on rye bread. Mexican huevos rancheros, a dish of beans, salsa, and eggs, has become a popular brunch staple in North America. Chinese dim sum brunch is a lively, noisy event, with servers navigating around tables wheeling carts laden with delicacies such as *char siu baau* (a bun with barbecued pork filling), dumplings, fried foods, and desserts. But eggs, as everyone knows, dominate the North American notion of a bountiful brunch, and eggs benedict tops the list of classic brunch favorites.

Brunch shouldn't be limited to special occasions and holidays, though, as it's been elevated to an art form and is the perfect opportunity to gather with family and friends to enjoy delicious food. *The World's 60 Best Brunch Dishes… Period* offers a diverse collection of classic brunch dishes, family-style comfort food, elegant offerings, and exciting recipes from across the globe, all easy to prepare and absolutely delicious!

MUST-HAVE TOOLS

FOR THE WORLD'S BEST BRUNCH DISHES

1. A large **non-stick pan** for cooking crêpes, frittatas, eggs, and röstis without a hassle

2. A sharp **chef's knife** for chopping, cubing, dicing, slicing, and mincing

3. A **whisk** for whipping, beating, and mixing

4. A **rolling pin** for rolling out pie crust dough, puff pastry, etc.

5. A **turning spatula** for flipping and manipulating fragile preparations

6. A **baking sheet** for baking and roasting in the oven

7. A **muffin tin** for muffins, single-serving frittatas and quiches, and mini versions of all your favorite foods

8. A **slotted spoon** for draining and turning poached eggs and fried foods

9. A **pie pan** for baking quiches, pies, and tarts

10. **Mixing bowls** of various sizes for mixing and whisking ingredients

11. A **ladle** for pouring crêpe and pancake batter into perfect rounds

12. A **hand blender** for making smoothies, mousses, and purées

13. A **casserole dish** for cooking casseroles and gratins

14. A **loaf pan** for baking homemade breads and cakes

15. A quality **pair of tongs** for flipping food

16. A **peeler** for peeling fruits and vegetables

17. A **flexible plastic spatula** for delicately folding ingredients together and for scraping out bowls

TIPS & TRICKS

FOR CREATING THE WORLD'S BEST BRUNCH DISHES

1. When planning your brunch menu, try to create a balance between sweet and savory, and light and rich. A tempting assortment of dishes will pull any sleepyhead out of bed!

2. Prep as many dishes as you can a day ahead. Make the pancake batter, cook the potatoes, muffins, and cakes, whip up dressings and sauces... When the morning comes, you can finish your dishes without feeling rushed, and really enjoy that first coffee of the day.

3. Keep your freezer stocked with fruit. Freeze fresh fruit when it starts to become overripe: spread chopped fruit or berries onto a baking sheet and freeze. When the fruit is completely frozen, transfer it to a resealable freezer bag and put it back in the freezer. Use it to make last-minute smoothies and fruit toppings for pancakes and waffles, and in muffins, cobblers, and breads.

4. Serve a variety of breads and pastries. Fresh bread is, of course, ideal, but if you can't make it to the bakery in the morning, buy it in advance, freeze it, and defrost it before serving. Some grocery stores and bakeries also sell frozen, unbaked bread and pastries; take whatever you need out of the freezer the night before and bake it in the morning, before brunch. After all, what could be more heavenly than the aroma of freshly baked goods?

5. A platter of fresh, sliced, ripe seasonal fruit rounds out any brunch table: it makes an elegant centerpiece, and guests can help themselves without having to cut, peel, or remove seeds. Plus, it provides a lighter option to balance out the richness of the heavier dishes.

6. There's nothing better than brunching with friends, and cocktails are just the thing to spice up your gathering. Offer coffee with a shot of sweet liqueur, pop open a bottle of rosé, mix sparkling wine and fresh fruit cocktails, or serve savory, spicy caesars. Choose light, refreshing drinks over rich, creamy blends to make sure your guests still have plenty of room for the main event!

7. Don't limit brunch to Sundays or special occasions! Brunch doesn't have to be a big deal—leave your pajamas on and prepare a spread for your family or roommates with whatever's in the fridge, or relish a long, leisurely, romantic brunch with your better half, simply enjoying each other's company and savoring every last morsel.

8. Without a doubt, the key to a successful, delicious brunch for a large group is sharing tasks. Have your guests pick up the basics, like bread, wine, cheeses, pâtés, and fruit, while you provide the mains. Or why not make it a potluck? Potlucks are the perfect occasion for exchanging recipes.

9. Finally, always remember that the best brunch dishes are made using the freshest ingredients.

HOW-TO GUIDE

Cooking eggs: it seems simple enough, but when it comes down to the details, cooking eggs can actually be quite tricky. Here are a few tips for making the perfect eggs, every time. And remember, practice makes perfect!

POACHED EGGS: Pour 1 tbsp vinegar into a large pot of water for every egg you'll be poaching. Bring the water and vinegar to a boil and then reduce the heat. With a spoon, swirl the simmering water to create a whirlpool. Crack the eggs, carefully, and one at a time, directly into the center of the whirlpool. Cook for 4 minutes and then remove with a slotted spoon. Plunge the eggs immediately into cold water to stop them from cooking.

SCRAMBLED EGGS: In a bowl, whisk the eggs vigorously and then season with salt and pepper. In a non-stick pan over medium heat, melt a bit of butter. Pour in the eggs and cook, stirring constantly with a wooden spoon. When the eggs are almost, but not completely set, take the pan off the heat and add 1 tsp cream per egg. Mix vigorously for a few seconds. The eggs stop cooking as soon as the cream is added, and will be wonderfully rich and creamy.

EGGS OVER EASY: In a non-stick pan over medium heat, melt a bit of butter, or use a bit of vegetable oil if you don't want your eggs to brown quite as much. Carefully break the eggs into the pan. When the whites have just set on the bottom, and you're sure they won't break, use a spatula to quickly flip them over (again, gently, so the yolks don't break). Cook until the whites are opaque but not completely set, testing for doneness by carefully tapping the yolks with the spatula (you want them runny on the inside). Avoid moving the eggs around too much in the pan, or the yolks will break.

SUNNY-SIDE-UP EGGS: Follow the technique for eggs over easy, but don't flip the eggs. Keep the heat at medium and keep a close eye on the egg yolk borders, where they join the whites. As soon as the whites around the yolks no longer look loose, the eggs are ready. Just remember: if the pan is too hot, the yolk bottoms will overcook and you'll lose that runny, creamy texture that's perfect for dipping toast. Sunny-side-up egg yolks are liquid gold!

SOFT-BOILED EGGS: Bring the eggs to room temperature to prevent the shell from cracking when you drop them into the water. Using a slotted spoon, carefully place the eggs in gently simmering water. Let simmer for 4 minutes. Drain the eggs and plunge them immediately into cold water to stop them from cooking.

HARD-BOILED EGGS: Follow the technique for soft-boiled eggs, but instead, cook the eggs for 11 minutes. Plunge the eggs immediately into cold water and peel them once they've cooled.

STORING EGGS: To preserve their freshness, eggs should always be stored in an airtight container. Eggs have porous shells and tend to absorb odors, so keep strong-smelling foods like onions and garlic on neighboring refrigerator shelves.

USING VINEGAR: Vinegar speeds up the coagulation of the egg proteins, which stops the egg from spreading through the water, resulting in beautifully round, perfectly poached egg whites enclosing creamy, runny yolks. Soft-boiled eggs also benefit from vinegar: it prevents the whites from leaking out if the eggshells happen to crack.

GLOSSARY

1. SEASON

To improve the flavor of a dish by adding salt and pepper to taste.

2. DICE

A basic knife cut in which food is cut into cubes.

3. THINLY SLICE

To cut into thin, equal slices.

4. CHOP

To cut into small pieces with a sharp instrument (knife or food processor).

5. SEAR

To cook in fat (butter or oil) at a high temperature to obtain a golden or brown crust.

6. ZEST

To remove the zest (outer skin) of citrus fruits with a zester, grater, or peeling knife.

7. SAUTÉ

To cook, stirring, over high heat in a pan, Dutch oven, or heavy-bottomed pot.

8. WILT

To cook certain vegetables (spinach, Swiss chard, kale, sorrel, etc.) over low heat, with or without a fat, in order to reduce their volume and release some of their liquid.

9. BLANCH

To cook vegetables briefly in boiling salted water.

10. ROLL OUT

To spread and flatten pastry or dough using a rol-ling pin. Lightly flour the work surface before rolling out your dough to prevent it from sticking.

11. BRUSH

To coat food with a thin layer of liquid or sauce using a brush or the back of a spoon.

12. WHIP

To vigorously beat a liquid, or a combination of liquids, until smooth. Whipping also incorporates air into a mixture (like whipped cream or meringue), making it light and fluffy.

THE CHEF'S SECRET

Every seasoned chef will attest that the real secret to creating a successful dish is to *taste! taste! taste!* Taste before and after seasoning, add some heat or a squeeze of lemon juice if you think your dish needs a little kick, or go ahead and double the herbs or even the cheese! The most important thing is to follow your instincts and your senses. Listen for that telltale sizzle, inhale the tantalizing aromas, and CONSTANTLY taste your food so you can get to know your dish in all its stages.

There you have it—the simple secret to creating delicious, original dishes.

THE GOOD MORNING BURGER

SERVES 4

INGREDIENTS

Meat from 2 sausages of your choice
2 tbsp vegetable oil
4 slices cheddar cheese
4 eggs
Salt and freshly ground pepper
1 tbsp butter
4 English muffins
2 tbsp mayonnaise
4 slices tomato

PREPARATION

Shape sausage meat into 4 patties. In a pan, heat vegetable oil and cook patties for about 3 minutes on each side. Top with cheddar cheese and set aside, but keep warm.

In a small bowl, whisk eggs together and then season with salt and pepper. In a pan, heat butter, pour in the egg mixture, and cook for 2 minutes. Divide into 4 equal portions, flip, and finish cooking.

Toast English muffins and then spread each muffin bottom with mayonnaise. Top with sausage patties, eggs, and tomato slices. Close burgers and serve.

CAFÉ MOCHA & CHAI WITH A KICK

MAKES 4 CUPS PER RECIPE

FOR CHAI TEA

3 teabags (black)
3 cups (750 ml) boiling water
1 cup (250 ml) milk
1 tbsp sugar
1 tsp cinnamon
1/2 tsp ground ginger
1/4 tsp ground cardamom
1 star anise
1 pinch ground nutmeg
3-1/2 oz Irish cream liqueur

FOR CAFÉ MOCHA

1/4 cup (60 ml) 35% cream
2 tbsp semi-sweet chocolate chips
1 lemon wedge
1/4 cup (60 ml) sugar
4-1/2 oz hazelnut liqueur
4 cups coffee
Dark or milk chocolate shavings

PREPARATION

For chai tea: Steep teabags in boiling water for 3 to 4 minutes, depending on how strong you like your tea. Discard bags and set tea aside.

In a small pot, combine milk, sugar, and spices. Bring to a boil, reduce heat, and let simmer, stirring constantly, for about 2 minutes.

Pour tea into 4 cups, add spiced milk, and top up each cup with Irish cream liqueur. Serve immediately.

For café mocha: Using an electric mixer, whip cream vigorously until soft peaks form.

Put chocolate chips into a small bowl and melt in the microwave for 15 seconds. If chocolate hasn't melted, heat for 15 seconds longer. Repeat until chocolate is completely melted, but not hot. Add chocolate to whipped cream, whipping vigorously until stiff peaks form. Refrigerate.

Rub the rims of 4 coffee cups with lemon. Spread sugar out in a saucer, flip the cups, and dip the rims in sugar to coat. Pour 2 tbsp hazelnut liqueur into each cup and then fill them with coffee. Top with chocolate whipped cream and a few chocolate shavings. Serve immediately.

THE CORNED BEEF HASH

SERVES 6

INGREDIENTS

2 yellow-fleshed potatoes (Yukon Gold)
1 tbsp butter
1 onion, finely chopped
1 tbsp fresh thyme, chopped
1 tin (12 oz) corned beef
1 egg
Freshly ground pepper
2 tbsp vegetable oil

PREPARATION

In a pot, cover potatoes with water and bring to a boil. Let simmer for 30 minutes over low heat. Drain, let cool, and peel.

In a pan, melt butter and sauté onion and thyme for 3 to 4 minutes. Set aside.

Grate potatoes into a bowl. Add corned beef, onion and thyme, and egg, and mix well. Season with salt and pepper.

In a large pan, heat oil and then add corned beef and potato mixture. Flatten it into a large, compact patty, or galette, and cook over medium heat for 8 to 10 minutes, until the underside is golden. Stir, flatten again, and cook for another 8 to 10 minutes.

Cover pan with a plate larger than the diameter of the pan. Turn the pan over and flip the galette onto the plate. Carefully slide it back into the pan, with the golden brown underside now on top. Cook for 10 minutes to brown the other side and then serve with eggs and confit tomatoes (see recipe on page 068) or sour cream.

DID YOU KNOW?

In the United States, September 27th is "National Corned Beef Hash Day."

BRANDADA DE BACALAO

SERVES 4

FOR BRANDADA

1 yellow-fleshed potato (Yukon Gold), peeled and cut into 8 pieces
2 cloves garlic, chopped
2 cups (500 ml) milk
1 lb fresh cod
2 tbsp fresh tarragon, chopped
1/4 cup (60 ml) olive oil
1/2 tbsp salt
Freshly ground pepper

FOR SPANISH SALSA

2 tbsp capers, drained and rinsed
8 Kalamata olives, pitted and roughly chopped
1 shallot, finely chopped
8 cherry tomatoes, quartered
1/2 cup (125 ml) cucumber, very finely diced
2 tbsp olive oil
1 tsp sherry vinegar
Baguette slices, toasted

PREPARATION

In a pot, combine potato, garlic, and milk and bring to a boil. Let simmer for 20 minutes over low heat. Add cod and continue cooking for 10 minutes. Remove from heat and strain. Discard the milky "broth" and then transfer cod and potato mixture back to pot. Add tarragon and lightly mash with a wooden spoon. Add olive oil in a slow, steady stream, stirring constantly. Season with salt and pepper.

In a small bowl, combine all salsa ingredients, except baguette. Set aside.

Scoop brandada into a large casserole dish, or individual oven-safe dishes, and broil until the top is lightly golden. Serve warm with salsa and toasted baguette.

DID YOU KNOW?

Cod, haddock, and plaice are the most commonly used fish in classic fish and chips.

MELT-IN-YOUR-MOUTH CHANTERELLES

SERVES 2

INGREDIENTS

1 ciabatta bun
20 chanterelle mushrooms, washed
2 tbsp butter
2 shallots, finely chopped
1/4 cup (60 ml) white wine
1/2 cup (125 ml) store-bought demi-glace, prepared
1/4 cup (60 ml) 35% cream
Salt and freshly ground pepper
2 tbsp fresh chives, finely chopped
2 eggs, poached

PREPARATION

Cut the larger chanterelles in half, leaving the smaller ones whole. In a large pan, melt butter and sauté shallots. Add chanterelles, cook for 1 minute, and add white wine. Reduce until the wine has completely evaporated and then add demi-glace and cream. Season with salt and pepper and reduce until sauce is velvety and coats the mushrooms beautifully. Remove from heat and stir in chopped chives.

Cut the ends off the ciabatta bun, slice bun in half, and toast until golden but still soft inside. Set aside.

Spoon mushrooms over toasted ciabatta and top with poached eggs. Break eggs right before serving: the creamy yolks will flow between the mushrooms, creating a heavenly, silky sauce.

BRUNCH PIZZA

SERVES 4

INGREDIENTS

12 small asparagus stalks
1 cup (250 ml) thick-cut bacon, cut into 1/4-inch pieces
1 portion homemade or store-bought pizza dough
1/4 cup (60 ml) 35% cream
1 cup (250 ml) Gouda cheese, grated
8 button mushrooms, thinly sliced
Salt and freshly ground pepper
4 eggs

PREPARATION

With your hands, snap off the tough bottom ends of the asparagus stalks (they will break naturally where the spears become tender). Cut stalks in half.

In a pan, sauté bacon for 4 to 5 minutes. Drain on paper towels and set aside.

Preheat oven to 500°F (250°C).

Roll out pizza dough into a 12-inch circular crust. Spread cream over the entire surface and then top with cheese, bacon, asparagus, and mushrooms. Season with salt and pepper.

Cook pizza on the bottom rack for 4 minutes. After 4 minutes, remove pizza from oven, break eggs over top, and cook for another 6 minutes. Slice and serve.

 TASTY TIP

To make the perfect pizza crust every time, follow the recipe in *The World's 60 Best Pizzas... Period*!

PORK & BEANS

SERVES 10

SOAK TIME: OVERNIGHT

INGREDIENTS

2 cups (500 ml) dried navy beans
1 onion, halved
6 slices bacon, chopped
2 tsp dry mustard
1 cup (250 ml) ketchup
1/2 cup (125 ml) molasses
1/2 cup (125 ml) cider vinegar
4 cups water
2 tsp salt
1 tsp pepper

PREPARATION

Soak navy beans overnight in 4 times their volume of water, in the refrigerator. Drain, and rinse beans well just before putting them into the pot.

In a Dutch oven, or heavy-bottomed oven-safe pot, combine beans with remaining ingredients. Cover and cook in a 250°F (125°C) oven for 5 hours, stirring every hour. If mixture becomes too thick, add a bit of water. Serve with eggs.

 **DID YOU KNOW?**

Dried beans will keep for up to one year, stored in a cool, dry place in an airtight container.

MELON PROSCIUTTO CUPS

MAKES 12 APPETIZERS

INGREDIENTS

4 slices prosciutto
1/4 cup (60 ml) goat cheese
1/2 cantaloupe
2 tbsp fresh mint, chopped

PREPARATION

Preheat oven to 400°F (200°C).

Carefully cut each prosciutto slice into 3 equal pieces, to make 12 pieces.

Line a mini muffin tin with the prosciutto pieces, shaping them into small cups. Bake for 15 minutes, until crispy. Let cool slightly.

Spoon a small dollop of goat cheese into each cup.

Using a melon baller, scoop out 12 small melon balls. Place a melon ball in each cup, on top of the cheese. Garnish with a sprinkling of fresh mint and serve as an appetizer.

 **DID YOU KNOW?**

Real Italian prosciutto, with the Protected Designation of Origin (PDO) label, is cured using only sea salt, without the use of nitrites, preservatives, or colorants.

9

SWEET & SAVORY CRÊPE CAKE

SERVES 8

 TASTY TIP

Make sure the filling layers are very thin and even, so that the cake doesn't shift or slide when you're slicing it, and to prevent the filling from oozing out the sides.

FOR BÉCHAMEL

2 tbsp butter
2 tbsp flour
1 cup (250 ml) milk
1 pinch ground nutmeg
Salt and freshly ground pepper

FOR CAKE

3 portions crêpe batter (see recipe for 1 portion on page 060)
6 thin slices smoked ham
6 thin slices Swiss cheese
1/2 cup (125 ml) homemade or store-bought applesauce
Apple slices
Brown sugar

PREPARATION

Make 12 crêpes of about equal size and thickness. Set aside.

For béchamel: In a small pot, melt butter, stir in flour, and cook for 1 minute. Add 1/4 cup (60 ml) milk and stir until it turns into a smooth paste. Slowly pour in remaining milk, whisking constantly to prevent lumps from forming. Bring to a boil, whisking constantly until mixture becomes thick. Remove from heat, add nutmeg, and season with salt and pepper. Mix well and set aside.

Preheat oven to 350°F (175°C).

To assemble cake, line a baking sheet with parchment paper and layer the ingredients in the following order, saving the nicest crêpe for the very top: crêpe, 2 ham slices, crêpe, 2 cheese slices, crêpe, 2 tbsp (30 ml) applesauce, crêpe, 2 tbsp béchamel. Repeat 3 times.

Garnish with a few apple slices and sprinkle with brown sugar. Bake for 20 minutes, slice, and serve.

PORTOBELLO RUSTICO STACKS

SERVES 4

FOR PORTOBELLOS

2 chicken thighs, with or without skin
4 cups chicken stock
1 tbsp olive oil
2 shallots, finely chopped
1 cup (250 ml) homemade or store-bought tomato sauce
2 chipotle peppers in adobo sauce (canned), chopped
Salt and freshly ground pepper
2 tbsp olive oil
1 tbsp balsamic vinegar
4 portobello mushroom caps
4 slices smoked Gouda cheese

FOR PANKO-FRIED POACHED EGGS

4 poached eggs, chilled (see "How-To Guide" on page 027)
1/4 cup (60 ml) flour
1 egg, beaten
1/2 cup (125 ml) panko (Japanese breadcrumbs)
Vegetable oil for frying
Salt

PREPARATION

In a pot, cover chicken thighs with chicken stock and bring to a boil. Cover and let simmer for 30 minutes over low heat. After 30 minutes, remove chicken and save the broth for future use. If necessary, remove chicken skin. Using a pair of forks, shred chicken. Set aside.

In a pan, heat olive oil and sauté shallots. Add shredded chicken, tomato sauce, and chopped chipotles. Let simmer over low heat for 10 to 15 minutes, or until the sauce is thick enough to coat the chicken. Season with salt and pepper.

Preheat oven to 350°F (175°C).

In a small bowl, combine olive oil and balsamic vinegar. Brush portobellos with the mixture and place on a baking sheet, gill sides up. Top each cap with a scoop of chicken mixture and a slice of Gouda; bake for 15 minutes.

While the mushrooms are in the oven, very delicately roll the poached eggs in flour, dip in egg, and then coat with panko. In a large pot, heat 1-1/2 inches of oil. When a bit of panko dropped into the pot starts to sizzle, the oil is ready. Carefully lower the eggs into the hot oil and briefly fry, using a slotted spoon to flip them as soon as the undersides start to become golden. Quickly cook the other sides until golden brown, and then remove from oil with the slotted spoon. Drain on paper towels and season with salt. Top each mushroom with a poached egg. Serve and enjoy!

DELUXE BREAKFAST POTATOES

SERVES 4

FOR POTATOES

2 Russet potatoes
2 tbsp vegetable oil
1 onion, finely chopped
1/2 red pepper, seeded and diced
2 tbsp fresh thyme, chopped
1 tbsp butter
2 tbsp fresh parsley, chopped

FOR SEASONING

1/2 tsp mild paprika
1/4 tsp cayenne pepper
1/4 tsp onion powder
1/4 tsp garlic powder
Salt and freshly ground pepper

PREPARATION

In a large pot, cover potatoes with water and bring to a boil. Let simmer for 30 minutes. Drain potatoes, let cool, and peel. Cut into 1-inch cubes and transfer to a large bowl.

In a small bowl, combine all seasoning ingredients and then add to potatoes. Toss to coat.

In a large non-stick pan, heat oil and sauté onion, red pepper, and thyme for 3 to 4 minutes. Add potatoes and butter and cook, without stirring, until potatoes are golden brown on the bottom, and then stir and continue cooking until potatoes are beautifully golden and crispy all over. Delicately stir in parsley and serve as a side dish.

 **DID YOU KNOW?**

Archaeologists have found evidence of potato cultivation in the Andes mountains dating back to 8,000 BCE, but the tuber wasn't introduced to Europe until the 16th century, after the Spanish conquest of the Inca Empire.

12

SCALLOPS, ARTICHOKES & BOUDIN

SERVES 4

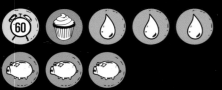

 DID YOU KNOW?

For as long as humans have been keeping animals to feed and clothe themselves, they have made some form of *boudin*, or black pudding. In fact, the first known recorded mention of the flavorful sausage is in Homer's epic poem *The Odyssey*, written around 1150 BCE, and the oldest written recipe for boudin can be found in *Apicius' De Re Coquinaria (The Art of Cooking)*, from about the 4th century CE.

INGREDIENTS

1/2 package (1 sheet) store-bought puff pastry
6 inches boudin noir sausage
1 tbsp butter
1 shallot, thinly sliced
4 artichoke hearts (in water), quartered
1/3 cup (80 ml) 15% cream
Juice of 1 lemon
1/2 cup (125 ml) baby scallops
Salt and freshly ground pepper

PREPARATION

Preheat oven to 350°F (175°C).

On a lightly floured work surface, roll out puff pastry into a square, about 1/4-inch thick. Cut into 4 equal squares. Place on a baking sheet lined with parchment paper and bake for 30 minutes.

While the pastry is in the oven, put the boudin sausage into a lightly oiled baking dish and cook in the oven for 15 minutes, or until fully cooked through. Remove from oven and let cool completely. Slice into 1/2-inch rounds.

In a pan over medium heat, melt butter and sauté shallot for 2 minutes. Add sliced boudin and continue cooking for 2 minutes, without stirring. Add artichoke hearts, cream, and lemon juice. Add scallops and stir gently. Cook for 1 minute, season, and remove from heat. Stir in parsley.

Split each puff pastry square into 2 layers. Place 1 layer on a plate, split side up, and top with a scoopful of scallop, artichoke and boudin mixture. Close sandwich with the other layer. Repeat with remaining ingredients and serve.

BLINTZES

SERVES 4

FOR CRÊPE BATTER (1 PORTION, MAKES 4 CRÊPES)

2 eggs
1 cup (250 ml) milk
1 tbsp sugar
1 pinch salt
A few drops vanilla extract
1 cup (250 ml) flour
1 tbsp butter

FOR FILLING

1 cup (250 ml) ricotta cheese
1 egg yolk
2 tbsp sugar
Juice of 1/2 lemon
2 tbsp butter, softened
1 tbsp butter, melted
Fruit purée or pure maple syrup

PREPARATION

To make the filling, line a wire mesh strainer with a paper towel and then rest the strainer over a bowl. Scrape ricotta cheese into the strainer, cover with plastic wrap, and place an unopened can of food on top to drain the excess liquid. Let sit for 20 minutes.

Meanwhile, make the crêpe batter by whisking together the eggs, milk, sugar, salt, and vanilla. Sprinkle in flour, whisking constantly to prevent lumps from forming. In a non-stick pan, melt a bit of butter and cook 4 crêpes, one at a time, adding another small pat of butter for each crêpe. Set aside.

In a bowl, whisk together drained ricotta, egg yolk, sugar, lemon juice, and softened butter, for 5 minutes.

Preheat oven to 400°F (200°C).

Place a crêpe on a flat work surface and spoon 1/4 cup (60 ml) filling into the center. Fold up all 4 sides to make a small square and then repeat with remaining ingredients. Transfer to a baking sheet, seam sides down, brush with melted butter, and bake for 15 minutes. Serve with fruit purée or maple syrup.

VEAL & CO.

SERVES 4

1-1/2 lbs veal flank steak
Sunny-side-up eggs (see "How-To Guide" on page 027)
Deluxe Breakfast Potatoes (see recipe on page 056)

FOR MARINADE

1/4 cup (60 ml) olive oil
2 tbsp balsamic vinegar
2 cloves garlic
4 sundried tomatoes
3 green onions
1/4 cup (60 ml) fresh parsley
1/4 cup (60 ml) fresh basil
Salt and freshly ground pepper

PREPARATION

In a food processor, purée all marinade ingredients.

In a large baking dish, pour marinade over veal and refrigerate for at least 2 hours.

Grill veal on the barbecue, or sear in a pan, for 2 minutes on each side. Let rest for 5 minutes, thinly slice, and serve with sunny-side-up eggs and Deluxe Breakfast Potatoes.

SAVORY BACON BREAD PUDDING

SERVES 6

INGREDIENTS

8 slices bacon, cut into 1-inch pieces
1 onion, finely chopped
1/2 loaf country bread, cut into 1-inch cubes
2 cups (500 ml) Gruyere cheese, grated
5 eggs
1/4 cup (60 ml) 35% cream
1 cup (250 ml) milk
1 tsp dry mustard
Salt and freshly ground pepper

PREPARATION

In a pan, sauté bacon and onion for 5 to 6 minutes, until completely cooked. Save bacon fat.

In a large bowl, combine cubed bread, bacon and onion mixture, bacon fat, and cheese.

Preheat oven to 350°F (175°C).

In a bowl, whisk together eggs, cream, milk, and mustard. Season with salt and pepper. Pour over bread mixture and mix well. Let sit for 10 minutes, stir again, and transfer to a greased baking dish. Bake for 25 minutes and serve nice and hot.

16

CONFIT TOMATOES

SERVES 4

INGREDIENTS

8 Italian tomatoes, halved, stem ends cut out
4 cloves garlic, thinly sliced
4 sprigs fresh thyme
4 sprigs fresh rosemary
1 tsp salt
1 tsp freshly ground pepper
1 tbsp sugar
1/2 cup (125 ml) olive oil

PREPARATION

Preheat oven to 275°F (135°C).

Arrange tomatoes on a baking sheet, cut sides up, and top each half with a slice of garlic. Scatter thyme and rosemary over halves and sprinkle with salt, pepper, and sugar. Drizzle generously with olive oil. Roast in the oven for 3 hours.

Serve with brunch instead of ketchup, as a gourmet condiment.

CLASSIC EGGS BENEDICT

SERVES 4

TASTY TIP

There are infinite variations of eggs benedict: try it with blanched asparagus, sautéed mushrooms, sliced Swiss cheese, smoked salmon, goat cheese, spinach, turkey, or even smoked meat. Make eggs benedict your way!

DID YOU KNOW?

Eggs benedict was invented in the United States, and was most likely loosely based on a New Orleans dish of puréed salt cod topped with a poached egg—in fact, the French term "à la bénédictine" actually applies to dishes made with salt cod!

FOR HOLLANDAISE SAUCE

1 cup (250 ml) butter
1/4 cup (60 ml) water
4 egg yolks
Cayenne pepper
Juice of 1/2 lemon
Salt and freshly ground pepper

FOR EGGS BENEDICT

8 slices back (Canadian) or regular bacon
4 English muffins
8 eggs, poached (see "How-To Guide" on page 027)

PREPARATION

For hollandaise sauce: In a small pot, melt butter over low heat. Using a spoon, skim the white foam from the surface. Remove pot from heat and let cool to room temperature (butter should still be liquid), before adding to sauce (instructions below).

In a bowl, over a bain-marie, whisk together water, egg yolks, and cayenne pepper until frothy. Remove from bain-marie and pour in melted butter in a slow, steady stream, whisking vigorously and constantly. Whisk in lemon juice and season with salt and pepper. Keep at room temperature. Right before serving, reheat over the bain-marie, whisking constantly, until warmed.

In a pan, cook bacon for a few minutes. Cut English muffins in half and toast. Top each muffin half with a slice of bacon, a poached egg, and a generous ladleful of sauce. Serve 2 per person.

PEACH & RICOTTA TART

SERVES 4

INGREDIENTS

1 cup (250 ml) ricotta cheese
2 tbsp sugar
1/4 tsp cinnamon
1/2 package (1 sheet) store-bought puff pastry
4 fresh peaches, pitted and cut into wedges
Icing sugar

PREPARATION

To make the filling, line a wire mesh strainer with a paper towel and then rest the strainer over a bowl. Scrape ricotta cheese into the strainer, cover with plastic wrap, and place an unopened can of food on top to drain the excess liquid. Let sit for 20 minutes.

In a bowl, vigorously and continuously whisk together ricotta cheese, sugar, and cinnamon, for 3 to 4 minutes, until mixture is creamy.

Preheat oven to 400°F (200°C).

On a flat, floured work surface, roll out puff pastry dough into a 12-inch square. Transfer to a lightly greased baking sheet. Spread ricotta mixture evenly over pastry and arrange peaches over top. Bake for 30 minutes, sprinkle with icing sugar, slice, and serve.

TASTY TIP

Drizzle with a bit of honey for just a hint of extra sweetness.

FUNKY FIJI CEVICHE

SERVES 4

INGREDIENTS

2 white fish fillets (tilapia, halibut, etc.), about 1 lb each, cut into 1/2-inch cubes
1/2 red onion, very thinly sliced
1/2 cup (125 ml) lime juice
1/2 jalapeño pepper, seeded and finely chopped
1/2 cup (125 ml) fresh cilantro, roughly chopped
1/2 cup (125 ml) fresh corn kernels
1/4 cup (60 ml) coconut milk
Salt and freshly ground pepper
Baguette, sliced

PREPARATION

In a bowl, combine fish, onion, and lime juice. Cover and refrigerate for 2 hours.

After 2 hours, drain fish and discard liquid. Add remaining ingredients, except bread, and mix well. Season with salt and pepper and refrigerate for 1 hour longer.

Serve cold with sliced baguette.

DOUGHNUT HOLES

MAKES 25 DOUGHNUT HOLES

INGREDIENTS

1 apple, grated
1 cup (250 ml) ricotta cheese
1 egg
1 tsp lemon juice
1/4 tsp cinnamon
2 tbsp sugar
1 tbsp baking powder
3/4 cup (180 ml) flour
Vegetable oil for frying
1/4 cup (60 ml) sugar

PREPARATION

In a large bowl, whisk together grated apple, ricotta cheese, egg, lemon juice, cinnamon, and baking powder. Gradually sprinkle in flour, whisking constantly to prevent lumps from forming.

Preheat oven to 400°F (200°C).

In a large pot, heat 2 inches of vegetable oil. When a bit of dough dropped into the oil starts to sizzle, the oil is ready. Using a pair of spoons, shape dough into small balls, about 1 tbsp each. Carefully drop doughnut holes into the oil, making sure not to overcrowd the pot (your doughnuts won't fry properly if they're too close together). Fry doughnuts, stirring frequently, until golden brown all over and then remove from oil using a slotted spoon and drain on paper towels. Transfer to a baking sheet and keep warm in the oven until all the doughnuts are cooked. Remove from oven, roll in sugar, and serve.

GOURMET GRAVLAX

SERVES 4

REST TIME: 24 HOURS

TASTY TIP

If you can find it, substitute 2 tbsp of smoked salt for the same quantity of coarse salt to give it a woodsy, earthy flavor.

DID YOU KNOW?

During the Middle Ages, fishermen prepared gravlax by heavily salting fish and then burying it in the sand to allow it to ferment. The name comes from joining the Swedish words *grav*, which means "grave," and *lax*, which means "salmon"; *gravlax* literally means "buried salmon." Today, gravlax is prepared by "burying" it in a mixture of sugar, salt, and dill.

FOR GRAVLAX

1/4 cup (60 ml) brown sugar
1/4 cup (60 ml) coarse salt
1 tbsp fennel seeds
1/4 cup (60 ml) fresh dill, chopped
1 tsp freshly ground black pepper
Zest of 1 lemon
1 lb fresh skinless salmon fillet, from the thinnest part of the fillet
2 tbsp gin

FOR SERVING

1/4 cup (60 ml) sour cream
1 tbsp honey
2 tbsp fresh dill, chopped
1/2 tsp Espelette pepper (optional)
4 slices rye bread, toasted

PREPARATION

In a bowl, combine brown sugar, salt, fennel seeds, dill, pepper, and lemon zest. Spread half of this mixture in the center of a large piece of plastic wrap, into a layer about the same size as the salmon fillet.

Rub salmon fillet with gin and place on top of brown sugar mixture. Cover with remaining mixture and another layer of plastic wrap. Wrap tightly, place in a dish or on a baking sheet, and refrigerate for 24 hours.

After 24 hours, unwrap fish and scrape off sugar mixture. Rinse fillet and dry thoroughly. Refrigerate, uncovered, for 1 hour, and then thinly slice.

In a bowl, combine sour cream, honey, dill, and Espelette pepper. Mix well.

Serve gravlax on toasted rye bread, garnished with sour cream topping.

22

BERLINERS

MAKES 15 BERLINERS

 **TASTY TIP**

If you don't have a stand mixer, give your arms a workout by kneading the dough by hand!

 DID YOU KNOW?

In many parts of Germany, these miniature filled doughnuts are called *Berliners*, although Berliners themselves call them *pfannkuchen!* In the American Midwest and parts of Canada, they're commonly known as bismarks.

FOR DOUGHNUT DOUGH

2-1/4 cups (560 ml) flour
1/4 cup (60 ml) sugar
1 tbsp fresh active yeast (also called compressed or cake yeast)
1 egg
8 tsp milk
1/3 cup (80 ml) water
2 tbsp butter, melted
Vegetable oil for frying

FOR GARNISH

1/2 cup (125 ml) strawberry jelly
1/4 cup (60 ml) icing sugar

PREPARATION

Using a stand mixer with the dough hook attachment, combine all doughnut dough ingredients on medium speed. Let mixer knead dough, about 8 minutes, or until dough is smooth. Remove dough from hook, form into a ball, and transfer to a lightly floured bowl. Cover dough and let rise in a warm place until doubled in size, about 1 hour.

Place dough on a lightly floured, flat work surface. Using a rolling pin, roll out dough to about 1/2 inch thick, sprinkling on more flour as needed to prevent dough from sticking. Using a round cookie cutter (about 3 inches in diameter), cut out doughnuts. Transfer to a baking sheet and let rise in a warm place for 30 minutes.

In a fryer, preheat oil to 315°F (160°C).

Gently place doughnuts in oil, and cook on both sides until golden brown. Remove with a slotted spoon and drain on paper towels. Using a chopstick, poke a hole into the side of each doughnut. Scoop jelly into a pastry bag fitted with a small tip and fill doughnut holes. Sprinkle with icing sugar and enjoy!

23

FRUITY SHRIMP SALAD

SERVES 4

FOR SALAD

1 cup (250 ml) Nordic shrimp
1 mango, peeled and cut into 1/2-inch cubes
1 apple, cut into 1/2-inch cubes
1/4 English cucumber, cut into 1/2-inch cubes
1/4 cup (60 ml) fresh cilantro, chopped
2 tbsp sesame seeds
Salt and freshly ground pepper

FOR VINAIGRETTE

1 tbsp rice vinegar
Juice of 1 lime
1 tsp sesame oil
1/4 cup (60 ml) vegetable oil

PREPARATION

In a salad bowl, combine all salad ingredients.

In a small bowl, combine all vinaigrette ingredients. Mix well and pour over salad. Toss well, adjust seasoning to taste, and serve.

CHICKEN LIVER MOUSSE

SERVES 6

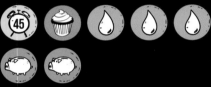

REST TIME: 2 TO 3 HOURS

 TASTY TIP

For a sophisticated presentation, pour the mousse into small espresso cups, cover with plastic wrap, and refrigerate until the mousse is set. Serve the cups on saucers with small knives for spreading.

INGREDIENTS

1 tbsp butter
4 chicken livers
2 shallots, thinly sliced
1/4 cup (60 ml) white port
1/2 cup (125 ml) red seedless grapes
1 tsp sherry vinegar
1/3 cup (80 ml) cold butter, cut into cubes
Salt and freshly ground pepper

PREPARATION

In a pan, heat 1 tbsp butter. Add chicken livers and cook for 1 to 2 minutes, undisturbed, until browned on the bottom. Add shallots,flip chicken livers, and continue cooking for 1 to 2 minutes. Deglaze with port and add grapes. Add vinegar and cook for 4 to 5 minutes over low heat. Remove from heat and let cool for 15 minutes.

In a food processor, or with a hand blender, purée liver mixture with its cooking juices, until smooth. Continue puréeing, adding cold butter cubes one at a time, and blend until completely smooth. Season with salt and pepper.

Line a large mold or several small molds with plastic wrap, to make it easier to unmold the mousse once it has set. Pour purée into the mold(s) and cover with plastic wrap, placing it directly on the surface of the mousse to seal.

Refrigerate for 2 to 3 hours. When mousse has set, serve with fresh or toasted bread.

SEASIDE STRATA

SERVES 6

REST TIME: 2 HOURS

INGREDIENTS

12 thin asparagus stalks
1/2 loaf sliced white bread, crusts removed
1/2 cup (125 ml) cream cheese
10 slices smoked salmon
1 cup (250 ml) old cheddar cheese, grated
5 eggs
1 cup (250 ml) 15% cream
1 tbsp Dijon mustard
Salt and freshly ground pepper

PREPARATION

With your hands, snap off the tough bottom ends of the asparagus stalks (they will break naturally where the spears become tender).

Line a loaf pan with parchment paper. Spread cream cheese onto bread slices, saving 2 plain slices for the top. Place a layer of bread and cream cheese at the bottom of the pan, cheese sides up. Top with 6 asparagus stalks and another layer of bread and cream cheese. Add a layer of smoked salmon, another layer of bread, and remaining asparagus. Finish with plain slices and top with grated cheese.

In a bowl, whisk together eggs, cream, and mustard. Season with salt and pepper and pour evenly over the bread, salmon, asparagus, and cheese. Cover with plastic wrap and refrigerate for at least 2 hours, or overnight. Bake in a 350°F (175°C) oven for 1 hour, flip out of pan, slice, and serve.

DID YOU KNOW?

The word strata actually means "layers": the perfect name for this dish!

26

CHIC SALMON EGGS BENEDICT

SERVES 2

INGREDIENTS

8 asparagus stalks
1 tbsp butter, melted
2 tbsp fresh dill, finely chopped
2 tbsp fresh chives, finely chopped
Salt and freshly ground pepper
2 English muffins
8 slices smoked salmon
1 recipe hollandaise sauce (see recipe on page 070)

PREPARATION

With your hands, snap off the tough bottom ends of the asparagus stalks (they will break naturally where the spears become tender). Blanch for 2 to 3 minutes in boiling water. Let cool and set aside.

Cut 4 squares of plastic wrap, 6 inches x 6 inches each. Brush the center of each square with melted butter. Sprinkle chopped dill and chives over buttered surfaces and then carefully place each square in a small bowl or teacup, pressing down gently to create hollows for the eggs. Gently crack eggs and tip into hollows. Carefully draw up the sides of the plastic wrap to make small parcels, and tie securely with kitchen string.

Bring a pot of water to a boil and gently drop in the eggs. Let simmer for 3 minutes and 30 seconds. Remove with a slotted spoon and let sit for 1 minute.

Slice asparagus stalks in half lengthwise and quickly warm in the microwave. Slice and toast English muffins and then top with asparagus and smoked salmon. Snip string on egg parcels and carefully tip out eggs onto the smoked salmon. Top with hollandaise sauce and serve.

TASTY TIP

Prepare the egg and plastic wrap parcels ahead of time to avoid any last-minute cooking disasters! And remember to add a generous splash of fresh lemon juice to your hollandaise sauce; citrus marries beautifully with asparagus and smoked salmon.

27

PUMPKIN CHOCOLATE CRUNCH MUFFINS

MAKES 12 MUFFINS

TASTY TIP

To make your own pumpkin purée, cut a pumpkin in half and place, cut side down, on a baking sheet. Bake in a 350°F (175°C) oven for 40 minutes. Scoop out the cooked pumpkin flesh, transfer to a food processor, and purée until smooth.

FOR MUFFINS

2 cups (500 ml) flour
1 tbsp baking powder
1 tsp baking soda
1/4 tsp salt
1 very ripe banana, puréed
1 cup (250 ml) homemade or store-bought pure pumpkin purée
1 egg
1/2 cup (125 ml) honey
1/4 cup (60 ml) butter, melted
1/2 tsp cinnamon
1/2 cup (125 ml) semi-sweet chocolate chips

FOR WALNUT CRUNCH TOPPING

1 cup (250 ml) walnuts, toasted and chopped
1/3 cup (80 ml) brown sugar
1/2 cup (125 ml) flour
3 tbsp butter, melted

PREPARATION

In a large bowl, combine flour, baking powder, baking soda, and salt. Make a well in the center and add puréed banana, pumpkin, egg, honey, butter, and cinnamon. Mix using a wooden spoon, until batter is smooth. Stir in chocolate chips.

Spoon batter into greased muffin cups, about 1/4 inch up the sides.

Preheat oven to 400°F (200°C).

To make the topping, combine nuts, brown sugar, and flour in a large bowl. Add melted butter and mix with a fork until the mixture has the texture of large crumbs. Top each muffin with a bit of the mixture and press lightly into batter. Bake for 18 to 20 minutes or until a toothpick inserted into the center of a muffin comes out clean. Remove from cups and serve.

28

WAFFLES

SERVES 8

TASTY TIP

Make decadent waffle "sandwiches": top a waffle with ham and cheese, close the "sandwich" with another waffle, and briefly bake them in the oven to melt the cheese. Garnish with a dollop of pear compote for a sweet and savory delight.

DID YOU KNOW?

The first commercial electric waffle maker was introduced in the United States in 1918, but it wasn't until the 1964 New York World's Fair that waffles, previously only popular in Europe, became a sensation on American soil.

FOR PEAR COMPOTE

4 pears, peeled, cored, and quartered
1/4 cup (60 ml) pure maple syrup
1 tsp lemon juice
2 tbsp butter

FOR WAFFLES

2 eggs
2 cups (500 ml) milk
1/2 cup (125 ml) butter, melted
2 cups (500 ml) sugar
2 tsp baking powder
Salt
1 tsp vanilla extract

PREPARATION

In a small pot, combine all pear compote ingredients. Cook for 30 minutes over low heat, stirring occasionally. Purée with a hand blender and set aside.

To make the waffles, separate eggs. Heat milk for 30 seconds in the microwave.

In a bowl, whisk together egg yolks and milk. Whisk in melted butter, and then gradually sprinkle in flour, whisking constantly. Add sugar, baking powder, salt, and vanilla. Mix until smooth.

In another bowl, using an electric mixer, beat egg whites until soft peaks form. Using a rubber spatula, delicately fold into egg yolk mixture to make the batter. Grease waffle maker with a bit of butter. Ladle batter onto the waffle maker (the amount will depend on the size of your waffle maker). Cook waffles until golden brown and serve with pear compote.

29

CRAB & MASCARPONE MINI QUICHES

MAKES 12 MINI QUICHES

INGREDIENTS

1 tbsp olive oil
4 green onions, thinly sliced
1 can (4-1/4 oz) crabmeat
1/2 cup (125 ml) corn
1/2 cup (125 ml) mascarpone cheese
8 eggs
Salt and freshly ground pepper
1 portion homemade or store-bought shortcrust pastry

PREPARATION

In a small pan, heat oil and sauté green onions for 3 to 4 minutes. In a bowl, combine crabmeat, green onions, and corn. Set aside.

In another bowl, whisk together mascarpone and eggs. Season with salt and pepper and set aside.

Preheat oven to 350°F (175°C).

On a flat, floured work surface, roll out dough to 1/4 inch thick. With a 4-inch cookie cutter, cut out pastry circles, and then carefully fit into the cups of a greased muffin tin. Spoon a bit of crab mixture into each cup, and then pour egg and mascarpone mixture over top.

Bake on the bottom rack for 25 to 30 minutes. Serve.

TASTY TIP

Instead of mini-quiches, make one large pie and serve it family-style (the cooking time will be slightly longer, about 30 to 40 minutes).

GRANOLA

MAKES 4 CUPS

INGREDIENTS

2 cups (500 ml) oats
1/2 cup (125 ml) sunflower seeds
2 tbsp flaxseeds
1/4 cup (60 ml) shredded unsweetened coconut
2 tbsp wheat germ
1 pinch salt
1/4 cup (60 ml) sunflower oil
1/4 cup (60 ml) honey
2 cups (500 ml) dried fruit, chopped (raisins, apricots, mangoes, dates, cranberries, etc.)

PREPARATION

Preheat oven to 325°F (165°C).

In a bowl, combine all ingredients, except dried fruit. Spread evenly onto a baking sheet lined with parchment paper and bake for 30 minutes, or until mixture is dried out and lightly golden. Let cool completely.

When mixture is cool, add dried fruit and stir. Store in an airtight container. Serve with yogurt and fresh fruit.

TASTY TIP

Toss in your favorite chopped nuts (almonds, pecans, cashews, etc.) before baking your granola to add a satisfying crunch!

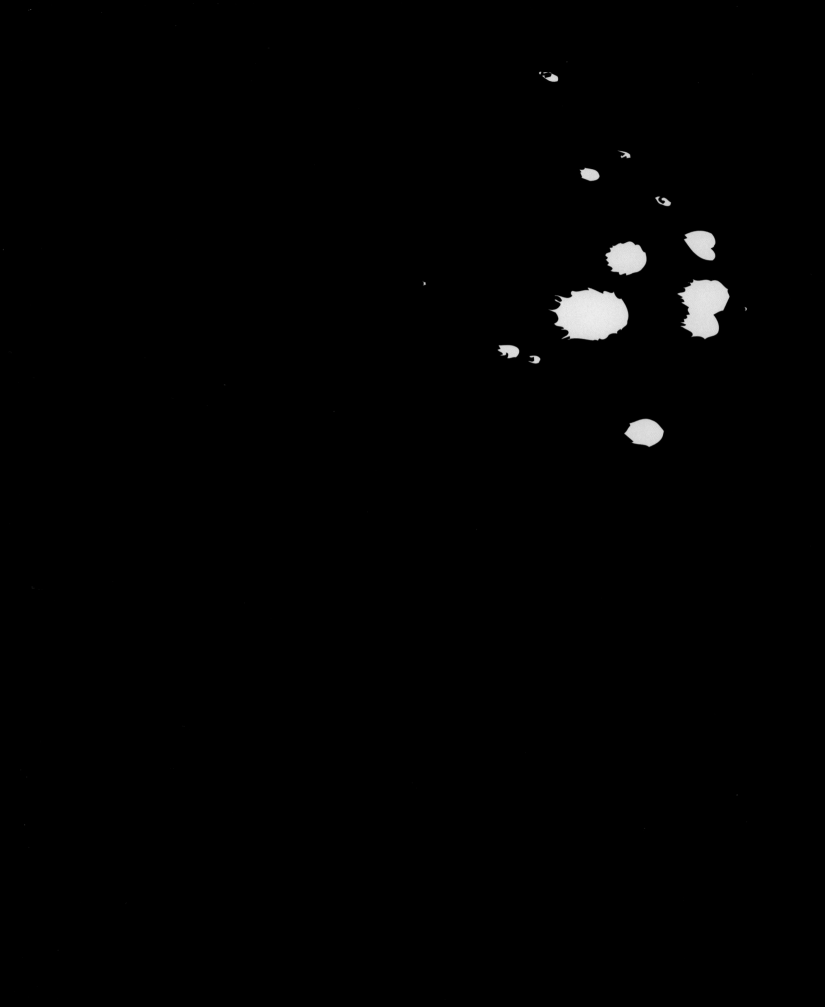

ALL-DRESSED BLINIS

MAKES 20 BLINIS

DID YOU KNOW?

Blinis were traditionally prepared by early Slavic peoples to celebrate *Maslenitsa*, in honor of the arrival of a new sun in spring, as their round shape represented the sun.

FOR BLINIS

1 egg
3/4 cup (180 ml) plain yogurt
1/4 cup (60 ml) milk
3/4 cup (180 ml) flour
1 tsp baking powder
Salt
1 tbsp butter

FOR GARNISH

10 quail eggs
1/4 cup (60 ml) cream cheese
10 slices smoked salmon
2 tbsp caviar or roe (lumpfish, sturgeon, salmon, etc.)
Espelette pepper
Sea salt

PREPARATION

In a bowl, whisk together egg, yogurt, and milk. Whisk in flour and baking powder. Season with salt and refrigerate for at least 30 minutes.

Bring a small pot of water to a boil. Using a slotted spoon, carefully place quail eggs in the boiling water. Let simmer for 4 minutes over low heat, drain, and plunge into ice water. Peel eggs and cut in half.

Heat a non-stick pan over medium heat and, using a paper towel, rub the surface of the pan with butter. Make small pancakes (about 1 tbsp batter each) and cook for 1 to 2 minutes, until undersides are golden brown. Flip and cook until golden brown. Repeat with remaining batter.

Spread a bit of cream cheese onto each blini and top with a half slice of smoked salmon, 1/4 tsp caviar or roe, and a quail egg half. Season egg with Espelette pepper and a sprinkling of sea salt. Serve.

TROPICAL TREATS

MAKES 16 SQUARES

FOR SQUARES

1/4 cup (60 ml) butter
2/3 cup (160 ml) sweetened condensed milk
60 social tea biscuits, finely crushed
1 cup (250 ml) shredded unsweetened coconut
2 cups (500 ml) dried fruit (apricots, mangoes, pineapple, papaya, etc.), roughly chopped
3 tbsp lemon juice

FOR LEMON ICING

2 tbsp butter, melted
2 tbsp hot water
3 tbsp lemon juice
3 cups (750 ml) icing sugar
1/2 cup (125 ml) dried fruit (apricots, mangoes, pineapple, papaya, etc.), roughly chopped

PREPARATION

In a pot, bring butter and condensed milk to a boil. Remove from heat and add crushed biscuits, coconut, dried fruit, and lemon juice. Mix well. Transfer to a 9-inch square baking pan lined with plastic wrap. Press down firmly to compact and refrigerate until set.

In a bowl, whisk together all icing ingredients, except dried fruit. When mixture is smooth, add fruit and mix well. Ice chilled square and refrigerate again, until icing is set. Cut into squares and enjoy!

THE KING OF GRILLED CHEESE

SERVES 4

INGREDIENTS

8 slices bacon
8 slices white bread
4 slices old cheddar cheese
2 bananas, sliced into rounds
1/4 cup (60 ml) peanut butter
1/4 cup (60 ml) butter, softened

PREPARATION

Place bacon on a baking sheet and cook in a 350°F (175°C) oven for 10 minutes. Drain on paper towels and set aside.

On a flat work surface, lay out 4 slices of bread and top with cheese, banana rounds, and bacon. Spread remaining slices of bread with peanut butter.

Close sandwiches and brush both sides with butter. Grill in a pan for a few minutes on each side, until golden brown. Slice and serve.

TASTY TIP

If you think this grilled cheese couldn't get any more decadent, try it with slices of fresh, buttery brioche bread!

DID YOU KNOW?

April is National Grilled Cheese Month!

IT'S NEVER TOO EARLY FOR BUBBLY

MAKES 1 COCKTAIL PER RECIPE

 **DID YOU KNOW?**

Champagne's characteristic bubbles are produced by adding several grams of yeast and sugar to each bottle. The yeast ferments and converts the sugar into alcohol; this allows carbon dioxide to form and create bubbles, which remain in the bottle until you pop the cork. The wire cage, or *muselet*, placed over the cork was invented in 1844 to prevent the cork from blowing out due to the pressure inside the bottle.

Today, champagne makers remove the dead yeast deposits (lees) that settle at the bottom of the bottles. This process is called disgorging; before this process was invented, champagne was cloudy—a far cry from the crystal clear liquid we drink today!

FOR CLASSIC MIMOSA

1/4 cup (60 ml) orange juice
1/4 cup (60 ml) sparkling wine

FOR LYCHEE GRAPEFRUIT MIMOSA

1 tbsp lychee liqueur
2 tbsp grapefruit juice
1 lychee, fresh or canned
1/4 cup (60 ml) sparkling wine

FOR STRAWBERRY BASIL MIMOSA

3 fresh strawberries, hulled and quartered
1 leaf fresh basil, chopped
6 tbsp sparkling wine

FOR CRANBERRY PEACH MIMOSA

1 tbsp peach liqueur
5 fresh raspberries
6 tbsp sparkling wine

PREPARATION

Place all ingredients, except sparkling wine, into a champagne flute. Add sparkling wine right before serving and enjoy with a lavish brunch!

THE PERFECT OMELET

MAKES 1 OMELET

INGREDIENTS

3 eggs
Salt and freshly ground pepper
1 tbsp fresh parsley, chopped
1 tsp fresh chives, chopped
1/2 tsp fresh thyme, chopped
1 tbsp butter
1 tbsp Gruyere cheese, grated
1 tbsp mozzarella cheese, grated
1 tsp goat cheese, crumbled

PREPARATION

In a bowl, whisk eggs for 30 seconds. Season with salt and pepper and add parsley, chives, and thyme. Whisk for 30 seconds to 1 minute longer.

In a small non-stick pan, melt butter over medium heat. When butter starts to bubble, add eggs. Let cook for 5 seconds, quickly mix with a rubber spatula, and then let set for a few more seconds.

Spread out cheese in the middle of the omelet. When the omelet is almost set, fold in half using a rubber spatula. Don't overcook! The omelet should still be slightly jiggly in the center, but not liquid. Slide onto a plate and serve with the side dish of your choice.

 **DID YOU KNOW?**

The expression "You can't make an omelet without breaking a few eggs" is a mid-19th century proverb attributed to Maximilien Robespierre, one of the most influential figures of the French Revolution. What it means, essentially, is that reaching a goal requires some measure of sacrifice.

36

SCRAMBLED EGG & FETA BITES

SERVES 2

INGREDIENTS

2 pitas
4 eggs
1 tbsp butter
Salt and freshly ground pepper
1 tbsp 35% cream
2 slices feta cheese (about 1/2-inch thick)
1/4 cup (60 ml) walnuts, toasted
1 cup (250 ml) fresh dill, chopped

PREPARATION

Slice pitas into triangles. Set aside.

In a small bowl, whisk eggs for 1 minute.

In a pan, melt butter over medium heat. Add eggs and cook, stirring constantly with a wooden spoon, until eggs are almost, but not completely, set. Remove from heat, add cream, and stir vigorously.

To serve, top each pita slice with a bit of egg, feta, walnuts, and dill. Fold up and eat!

CARAMEL COFFEE CAKE

SERVES 8

FOR TOPPING

1 tbsp cinnamon
2 tsp vanilla extract
1/2 cup (125 ml) walnuts, roughly chopped
8 store-bought soft caramels, quartered
1/2 cup (125 ml) sugar

FOR CAKE

2 cups (500 ml) flour
2 tsp baking powder
1 tsp baking soda
1/2 cup (125 ml) butter, brought to room temperature and cut into cubes
1 cup (250 ml) sugar
2 eggs
1 cup (250 ml) sour cream

PREPARATION

In a bowl, combine all topping ingredients. Set aside.

To make the cake, butter a tube pan. In a bowl, combine flour, baking powder, baking soda, and salt. Set aside.

Preheat oven to 350°F (175°C).

In another bowl, using an electric mixer, cream together butter, sugar, and eggs until smooth. Alternately add flour and sour cream in small amounts, mixing constantly. Pour half of the cake batter into the tube pan and then sprinkle with half of the topping. Add remaining batter and top with remaining topping. Bake for 30 to 35 minutes on the middle rack, until a toothpick inserted into the center comes out clean. Slice and serve with tea or coffee.

 **DID YOU KNOW?**

If you don't have a tube or bundt pan, use a springform pan with a buttered ramekin placed in the center.

PANETTONE FRENCH TOAST

SERVES 4

INGREDIENTS

1/2 cup (125 ml) milk
1/4 cup (60 ml) brown sugar
3 eggs
1/4 tsp vanilla extract
1/4 tsp cinnamon
2 tbsp butter
4 mini panettones, halved

PREPARATION

In a large bowl, combine all ingredients, except butter and panettones. Mix well.

Preheat oven to 350°F (175°C).

Melt butter in a large, non-stick pan. Dip panettone halves in the egg mixture for a few seconds and then place in the pan, flat sides down. Cook for 1 to 2 minutes over medium heat, until golden brown. Flip and cook the rounded sides, trying to brown them as much as possible. Transfer to a baking sheet and cook for 5 minutes in the oven.

Serve with crème fraîche, oranges, caramel sauce, or vanilla ice cream.

 **DID YOU KNOW?**

Italian bakeries produce over 200 million of these sweet cylindrical bread loaves every Christmas.

39

THE BEST SUNDAY HAM

SERVES 12

INGREDIENTS

1/4 cup (60 ml) honey
1 cup (250 ml) apple juice
1/2 cup (125 ml) brown sugar
1/2 tsp ground cloves
1/2 tsp freshly ground pepper
2 bay leaves
1 bone-in pork shoulder picnic ham (about 6-1/2 lbs)
1 bottle (12 oz) brown beer

PREPARATION

In a small pot, combine honey, apple juice, and brown sugar. Add cloves, pepper, and bay leaf. Bring to a boil and let simmer for 8 to 10 minutes over low heat, or until the mixture becomes thick, with the texture of a caramel glaze.

With a small knife, score a diamond pattern over the entire surface of the ham.

Place ham in a roasting pan and pour beer over top. Brush with glaze.

Cover and cook for 1 hour and 30 minutes in a 300°F (150°C) oven. After 1 hour and 30 minutes, remove cover and cook for 1 hour longer, basting ham often with its cooking juices and brushing it frequently with glaze. Slice and serve.

TASTY TIP

Replace the honey and brown sugar with 1 cup (250 ml) maple syrup for a classic French Canadian version!

DID YOU KNOW?

In the 1930s, popular ham glaze ingredients included ginger ale, marshmallows, pineapple, and pickle brine!

GOAT CHEESE, CRANBERRY & PISTACHIO POPPERS

MAKES 12 POPPERS

INGREDIENTS

1/2 cup (125 ml) goat cheese
1/4 cup (60 ml) shelled pistachios, toasted and chopped
1/4 cup (60 ml) dried cranberries, finely chopped
1 tbsp honey

PREPARATION

To prevent cheese from sticking, lightly moisten your hands before making the cheese balls. Roll goat cheese into small balls and refrigerate until firm.

In a bowl, combine pistachios and cranberries. Roll goat cheese balls in the mixture.

Serve with toothpicks and a dash of honey.

If you wish, keep the goat cheese whole and roll the entire log in the cranberry and pistachio mixture. Serve with toasted baguette.

DELIGHTFUL, DUNKABLE CHEESE STRAWS

SERVES 4

4 eggs
2 tbsp vinegar

FOR PARMESAN TRUFFLE CHEESE STRAWS

1 egg yolk
Salt and freshly ground pepper
1 tsp truffle oil
1/2 package (1 sheet) store-bought puff pastry
1/4 cup (60 ml) fresh Parmesan cheese, finely grated

FOR ARTICHOKE DIP

4 artichoke hearts, drained and rinsed
1 tbsp fresh rosemary leaves
1/4 cup (60 ml) olive oil
Salt and freshly ground pepper

PREPARATION

Preheat oven to 400°F (200°C).

For cheese straws: In a bowl, whisk together egg yolk, salt and pepper, and truffle oil.

On a lightly floured, flat work surface, roll out puff pastry into a square, about 1/4 inch thick. Brush with egg mixture and sprinkle with Parmesan cheese. Cut into 1/2-inch strips. Twist and place, side-by-side, on a baking sheet lined with parchment paper. Bake for 30 minutes, or until straws are golden brown. Let cool on a baking rack.

For artichoke dip: In a food processor, purée artichoke hearts and rosemary. Add oil in a slow, steady stream, puréeing until dip is creamy. Season with salt and pepper. Set aside.

Before cooking eggs, bring to room temperature. Bring a large pot of water to a boil, add vinegar, and carefully add eggs. Let simmer for 4 minutes over low heat, drain, and, with a small knife, slice off the top of each eggshell. Place in egg cups and serve with cheese straws and artichoke dip.

DID YOU KNOW?

The French have two slightly different methods of cooking soft-boiled eggs. Eggs cooked *"à la coque"* are boiled only for about three minutes, just enough time to slightly harden the white but leave the yolk warm and liquid, and are eaten straight out of the shell with a spoon. *"Mollet"* eggs are still soft, but are cooked for around six minutes, resulting in creamy yolks and whites that are firm enough to be easily peeled.

SEAFOOD CRÊPES

SERVES 4

DID YOU KNOW?

In spite of its name, buckwheat isn't related to wheat at all—it's actually related to sorrel and rhubarb. Because it's naturally gluten free, buckwheat flour is a safe, healthy alternative to wheat flour for people with gluten allergies. The buckwheat flower produces a dark, strong honey with a molasses-like flavor.

In Brittany, France, a popular street food is *galette saucisse*, fresh grilled sausage wrapped in a buckwheat crêpe and served from market carts.

FOR CRÊPE BATTER

2 eggs
1-1/2 cups (375 ml) milk
1 cup (250 ml) buckwheat flour
1/4 tsp salt
2 tbsp butter, melted

FOR SERVING

1 tbsp butter
4 eggs
8 slices Gouda cheese
1/2 cup (125 ml) Nordic shrimp
8 leaves fresh basil, chopped

PREPARATION

In a large bowl, whisk together eggs and milk. Gradually sprinkle in flour, whisking constantly to prevent lumps from forming. Add salt and melted butter. Mix well and refrigerate for at least 30 minutes.

Preheat oven to 300°F (150°C).

With a paper towel, coat a non-stick pan with butter. Over medium heat, pour a small amount of batter into the pan, swirling the pan to distribute the batter quickly and evenly to make a thin crêpe. Don't flip! Crack an egg into the center and gently mix. Top with 2 slices of cheese, a few shrimp, and a sprinkling of basil. Fold the edges in to make a square. Transfer to a baking sheet and keep warm in the oven, while you're cooking the other crêpes. Serve hot.

CINNAMON SUGAR ACCORDION BREAD

SERVES 6

FOR DOUGH

2 tbsp unsalted butter
1/2 cup (125 ml) milk
2-1/4 tsp instant yeast
1/4 cup (60 ml) sugar
1 ripe banana, puréed
1 tsp salt
2-1/2 cups (625 ml) flour

FOR CINNAMON SUGAR CARAMEL

1 cup (250 ml) brown sugar
2 tsp cinnamon
1/4 cup (60 ml) butter, melted

PREPARATION

In a pan, melt butter and cook until it starts to brown slightly. Remove from heat and add milk. Add yeast and sugar to warm milk and butter mixture and let sit for 10 minutes to activate yeast.

Transfer to a bowl and add banana, salt, and 2 cups (500 ml) flour. Knead for 8 minutes, until dough is stretchy and moist. If dough is too sticky, add flour 1 tbsp at a time. Transfer to a lightly greased bowl, cover with a towel, and let rise in a warm place for 1 hour and 30 minutes.

In a small bowl, combine brown sugar and cinnamon.

Preheat oven to 350°F (175°C).

On a flat, floured work surface, knead dough for 30 seconds and then roll out into a 16-inch x 12-inch rectangle. Brush with melted butter and top with cinnamon and brown sugar mixture.

Cut dough vertically into 4 strips, about 4 inches x 12 inches each, and stack them. Slice the stack into 3 squares, about 4 inches x 4 inches each, and stack again. Place the stack on its side in a buttered 4-inch x 8-inch loaf pan, cover with a towel, and let rise in a warm place for 30 minutes. Bake for 30 to 40 minutes, or until bread is golden brown. Turn out of the pan and brush with melted butter. Serve.

STUFFED DATES

MAKES 8 DATES

INGREDIENTS

8 Medjool dates
2 tbsp goat cheese
8 pecans, toasted
4 slices bacon
1 tbsp olive oil
1 tbsp sherry vinegar

PREPARATION

Using a small knife, carefully slice a small cut into each date and remove the pits. Stuff each date with a bit of cheese and a pecan. Close. Cut bacon slices in half. Tightly wrap dates in bacon.

In a non-stick pan, heat oil and sear dates, with the edges of the bacon facing down. Cook, turning often, to brown bacon. When bacon is browned, pour in vinegar and delicately stir to coat dates.

Pierce each date with a toothpick and serve as appetizers.

 **TASTY TIP**

For an equally delicious alternative, substitute the goat cheese with blue cheese, and the pecans with whole walnuts.

OVEN-BAKED APPLE CINNAMON PANCAKE

SERVES 4

FOR PANCAKE

3 eggs
1/3 cup (80 ml) milk
2 tbsp brown sugar
1/4 tsp cinnamon
1/3 cup (80 ml) flour
1 tsp baking powder

FOR TOPPING

2 tbsp butter
2 tbsp brown sugar
3 apples, peeled, cored, and thinly sliced into wedges
1/4 cup (60 ml) golden raisins

PREPARATION

In a large bowl, whisk together eggs, milk, brown sugar, and cinnamon. Gradually sprinkle in flour, whisking constantly to prevent lumps from forming. Whisk in baking powder and set aside.

Preheat oven to 400°F (200°C).

In a large, oven-safe pan, melt butter and brown sugar. Add apples and raisins and cook for 5 to 6 minutes, until apples are golden. Pour batter over top, gently stir, and bake in the oven for 10 minutes. Slice and serve with maple syrup.

 TASTY TIP

Add thinly sliced ham along with the apples. After taking the cake out of the oven, slice it up, place the slices on a baking sheet, and top with grated Gruyere cheese. Broil for a few minutes and then serve for a protein-packed meal in no time at all!

HUEVOS RANCHEROS

SERVES 4

FOR SAUCE

1 shallot, chopped
1 can (28 oz) diced tomatoes, drained
1 jalapeño pepper, seeded and finely chopped
1/2 tsp cumin
2 tbsp olive oil
1/4 cup (60 ml) fresh cilantro, chopped
Salt and freshly ground pepper
Hot sauce to taste

FOR TORTILLA STRIPS

2 medium tortillas
2 tbsp olive oil
Salt

FOR HUEVOS RANCHEROS

2 cups (500 ml) homemade sauce (see recipe above)
1 cup (250 ml) canned black beans, drained and rinsed
4 eggs
Salt and freshly ground pepper
2 tbsp 35% cream
1/2 cup (125 ml) Monterey jack cheese, grated

PREPARATION

In a bowl, combine all salsa ingredients. Mix well.

Slice tortillas into thin strips. In a bowl, combine strips with olive oil and salt. Spread onto a baking sheet and bake in a 350°F (175°C) oven for 10 minutes, or until tortilla strips are crispy and golden brown.

Pour salsa and beans into a large pan and let simmer gently. Make 4 hollows in the mixture and crack an egg into each one. Season with salt and pepper and then pour cream over eggs. Sprinkle with grated cheese, cover, and cook for 4 to 5 minutes over low heat. Serve with tortilla strips.

DID YOU KNOW?

Huevos rancheros is a popular Mexican breakfast dish traditionally served to farm workers as a mid-morning meal.

BRUNCH GREENS

SERVES 4

FOR CRANBERRY VINAIGRETTE

3 tbsp canned cranberry sauce
2 tbsp honey
1 tsp Dijon mustard
1 tbsp balsamic vinegar
1/2 cup (125 ml) grapeseed oil

FOR SALAD

4 cups mesclun salad mix
1/4 cup (60 ml) almonds, toasted and roughly chopped
1 orange, segmented, pith and membranes removed
1 grapefruit, segmented, pith and membranes removed
2 tbsp dried cranberries

PREPARATION

In a small bowl, whisk together cranberry sauce, honey, mustard, and vinegar. Add oil in a slow, steady stream, whisking constantly, until vinaigrette is creamy.

In a salad bowl, combine all salad ingredients. Toss with dressing right before serving.

TASTY TIP

Make homemade cranberry sauce by combining 1/2 cup (125 ml) sugar, 1/2 cup (125 ml) brown sugar, 1/2 cup (125 ml) orange juice, 1/2 cup (125 ml) water, and 3-1/4 cups (12 oz) fresh or frozen cranberries in a pot. Bring the mixture to a boil, let it simmer for 20 minutes, and then purée into a smooth sauce.

SALMON, MAPLE & BACON BITES

MAKES 12 BITES

INGREDIENTS

4 slices bacon
1/4 cup (60 ml) pecans, toasted and roughly chopped
1 lb salmon
1/4 cup (60 ml) sugar
2 tbsp butter
2 tbsp sherry vinegar
1/4 tsp sea salt

PREPARATION

Preheat oven to 350°F (175°C).

Place bacon on a baking sheet and cook in the oven for 15 minutes, or until crispy. Drain on paper towels and then roughly chop. In a small bowl, combine chopped bacon and pecans.

Cut salmon into 1-inch cubes. Bring a pot of water to a boil. Add salmon and cook for 20 seconds. Drain and then arrange on a baking sheet lined with parchment paper. Let cool.

In a small pot, melt sugar. Cook over medium heat until it turns into a caramel. When it starts turning golden brown, remove from heat and stir in butter. Add vinegar, salt, and bacon and pecan mixture. Put back on the stovetop and cook for 1 to 2 minutes, stirring constantly. Top each salmon piece with a spoonful of bacon pecan caramel. Refrigerate for at least 10 minutes. Serve cold.

JALAPEÑO CORNBREAD

SERVES 10

INGREDIENTS

1-1/4 cups (310 ml) flour
1-1/4 cups (310 ml) cornmeal
5 tsp baking powder
1/4 tsp salt
1/2 cup (125 ml) honey
1-1/4 cups (310 ml) buttermilk
1 egg
1 tsp butter, melted
1 cup (250 ml) fresh corn kernels
1 jalapeño pepper, seeded and finely chopped

PREPARATION

In a large bowl, combine flour, cornmeal, baking powder, and salt.

In another bowl, whisk together honey, buttermilk, and egg. Pour into dry mixture and mix until smooth. Add melted butter, corn, and jalapeño pepper; don't overmix.

Preheat oven to 325°F (165°C).

Pour batter into a non-stick loaf pan, buttered or lined with parchment paper. Bake for 45 minutes, or until a toothpick inserted into the center comes out clean. Tip out of the pan and let cool for 10 minutes before slicing. Serve with butter.

 DID YOU KNOW?

Cornbread is a truly authentic American dish: before the arrival of European explorers, Native Americans had been using ground corn, or maize, to make flour for thousands of years. European settlers learned the process of grinding corn, and soon invented their own recipes for cornmeal breads, which were usually cooked in a skillet over the fire.

SPINACH, SUNDRIED TOMATO & FETA QUICHE

SERVES 4

INGREDIENTS

1 tbsp olive oil
1 onion, finely chopped
2 cups (500 ml) broccoli, cut into small florets
2 tbsp sundried tomatoes, thinly sliced
2 cups (500 ml) spinach
1 portion homemade or store-bought shortcrust pastry
1/2 cup (125 ml) feta cheese, crumbled
4 eggs
1/2 cup (125 ml) milk
Salt and freshly ground pepper

PREPARATION

In a large pan, heat olive oil and sauté onion for 1 to 2 minutes. Add broccoli and sundried tomatoes and continue cooking for 2 to 3 minutes. Add spinach, stir, and cook for 2 minutes. Set aside.

Preheat oven to 375°F (190°C).

On a flat work surface, roll out dough and fit into a 9-inch greased pie pan. Spread half of the feta cheese over crust bottom and top with vegetable mixture. Sprinkle with remaining feta.

In a bowl, whisk together eggs and milk. Season with salt and pepper and pour evenly into the pie crust. Bake on the bottom rack for 30 minutes. Let cool for at least 10 minutes before serving.

BREAKFAST CASSEROLE

SERVES 4

FOR GRUYERE BÉCHAMEL SAUCE

2 tbsp butter
2 tbsp flour
1 cup (250 ml) milk
1 cup (250 ml) Gruyere cheese, grated
Salt and freshly ground pepper

FOR CASSEROLE

2 potatoes, peeled and cut into 1/2-inch cubes
1 onion, finely chopped
12 mushrooms, quartered
2 tbsp fresh oregano, chopped
2 tbsp olive oil
Salt and freshly ground pepper
2 mild sausages
4 to 8 eggs

PREPARATION

Preheat oven to 400°F (200°C).

In a bowl, combine potatoes, onion, mushrooms, oregano, and oil. Season with salt and pepper and spread onto a baking sheet. Place whole sausages over top and bake for 40 minutes in the oven.

For gruyere béchamel sauce: In a pot, melt butter. Add flour and cook for 1 minute. Whisk in 1/4 cup (60 ml) milk, and stir until it turns into a smooth paste. Slowly pour in remaining milk and bring to a boil, whisking constantly to prevent lumps from forming. Continue cooking and whisking until sauce becomes thick. Add cheese, season with salt and pepper, and remove from heat.

When potato mixture and sausages are cooked, slice sausages, combine with potato mixture, and transfer to individual oven-safe dishes. Spoon béchamel over top. Crack 1 or 2 eggs over each and bake in a 350°F (175°C) oven for 15 minutes. Serve hot.

SIMPLY GOOD FRIED PLANTAINS

SERVES 2

INGREDIENTS

1 ripe plantain
Vegetable oil for frying
Juice of 1 lime
Sour cream

PREPARATION

Peel plantain and slice into 1/2-inch pieces, on the diagonal.

Pour vegetable oil into a large pot, about 1 inch up the sides. When the oil starts to sizzle when a plantain slice is dropped in, the oil is ready. Carefully arrange slices in the oil and fry until the undersides are golden brown. Flip and continue cooking until golden brown. Remove from oil with a slotted spoon and drain well on paper towels.

Transfer fried plantain to a plate and drizzle lime juice over top. Serve with sour cream and toast.

 DID YOU KNOW?

Plantains have a lower sugar content than the "dessert" bananas we love to snack on, and are usually cooked before eating. They are a staple food in the tropical regions of the world, especially in developing countries, as they can be grown year-round.

CAESAR OYSTERS

MAKES 12 OYSTERS

INGREDIENTS

1 Italian tomato
12 fresh oysters, thoroughly cleaned
Tabasco sauce
Juice of 1 lemon
2 tbsp fresh cilantro, chopped
Celery salt
Coarse salt

PREPARATION

Cut out tomato stem. Grate tomato into a bowl and then drain with a wire mesh strainer to remove the liquid. Discard liquid and set grated tomato aside.

Shuck oysters with an oyster knife. Slide knife under the muscles to loosen meat. Place on a bed of coarse salt to stabilize.

Garnish each oyster with a drop of Tabasco sauce, a dash of lemon juice, 1 tsp grated tomato, and a bit of cilantro. Finish with a sprinkling of celery salt and serve immediately.

DID YOU KNOW?

The Ceasar was invented in Calgary, Canada in 1969, and is typically made with vodka, a tomato and clam juice blend, hot sauce, and Worcestershire sauce. Restaurateur Walter Chell created the drink for the opening of a new Italian restaurant, and was inspired by *spaghetti alle vongole*, an Italian dish of pasta, tomatoes, and clams.

BLUEBERRY PANCAKES

MAKES 12 PANCAKES

INGREDIENTS

4 eggs
2 tbsp sugar
2 cups (500 ml) buttermilk
1/4 tsp salt
2 cups (500 ml) flour
2 tbsp baking powder
2 tbsp butter, melted
2 tbsp butter (for cooking)
1 cup (250 ml) fresh or frozen blueberries

PREPARATION

In a bowl, whisk together eggs, sugar, buttermilk, and salt. Gradually sprinkle in flour and mix until smooth, whisking constantly to prevent lumps from forming. Add baking powder and melted butter. Refrigerate for 10 minutes.

Using a paper towel, grease a non-stick pan with butter and heat over medium heat. Ladle batter into pan to make 4-inch rounds. Sprinkle blueberries onto the surface of each pancake. When pancakes are golden brown on the underside, flip and then continue cooking until golden brown. Repeat with remaining batter.

Serve immediately, or cover and keep warm in the oven. Top with maple syrup, caramel, whipped cream, or more butter.

 DID YOU KNOW?

What's the difference between crêpes and pancakes? Crêpes originated in Brittany, France, and are generally large in diameter and fairly thin, ideal for wrapping around sweet or savory fillings. The popular American breakfast pancakes are smaller in diameter and rise to become thick and fluffy.

55

SMOOTHIES RULE!

SERVES 4 PER RECIPE

FOR CREAMY MANGO SMOOTHIE

2 cups (500 ml) fresh or frozen mango, cubed
1 cup (250 ml) vanilla yogurt
1 cup (250 ml) milk
Juice of 1 lime

FOR BERRY BANANA SMOOTHIE

2 ripe bananas, cut into rounds
1 cup (250 ml) fresh or frozen berries
2 cups (500 ml) soy milk

FOR TROPICAL SMOOTHIE

2 cups (500 ml) orange juice
2 cups (500 ml) fresh or frozen pineapple, cubed
1 tbsp fresh ginger, peeled and grated
1/2 cup (125 ml) coconut milk

FOR STRAWBERRY PROTEIN SMOOTHIE

1 cup (250 ml) soft tofu
2 cups (500 ml) fresh or frozen strawberries
1/4 cup (60 ml) pure maple or cane syrup
1 cup (250 ml) water or crushed ice

PREPARATION

In a blender, purée smoothie ingredients. Serve in a pitcher, or in pretty glasses.

GRUYERE & ROSEMARY RÖSTI

SERVES 6

INGREDIENTS

2 Russet potatoes
1 cup (250 ml) Gruyere cheese, grated
2 tbsp fresh rosemary, chopped
2 tbsp fresh parsley, chopped
1 tsp salt
1/2 tsp freshly ground black pepper
2 tbsp butter

PREPARATION

In a pot, cover potatoes with water and bring to a boil. Let simmer for 30 minutes. Drain, let cool, and peel.

In a bowl, grate potatoes and combine with cheese and herbs. Season with salt and pepper and mix well. Shape into flat patties, about 3 inches in diameter and 1/2-inch thick.

Melt butter in a non-stick pan. Arrange potato patties in the pan and cook for 5 to 6 minutes, or until undersides are golden brown. Flip and cook the other sides, until golden. Serve with eggs and meat of your choice.

 TASTY TIP

Rösti are very delicate, so try not to move them around too much in the pan. Let them cook, undisturbed, until golden brown on the bottom, and then flip them to brown the other side.

 DID YOU KNOW?

Rösti, or röschti, are typically only eaten by the German-speaking part of Sweden. The Swedish jokingly refer to the line separating the French- and German-speaking sides as the *Röstigraben*, or "rösti ditch."

HAM & EGG NESTS

SERVES 4

INGREDIENTS

2 cups (500 ml) baby spinach
1/4 cup (60 ml) water
4 mini bread loaves, or crusty buns
1/4 cup (60 ml) cream cheese
4 slices smoked ham, cut into strips
Salt and freshly ground pepper
4 eggs

PREPARATION

Preheat oven to 350°F (175°C).

In a pan, wilt spinach in water. Drain well.

With a knife, cut a circle out of the top of each mini loaf and scoop out the soft bread inside to make a cavity for stuffing.

Spoon 1 tbsp cream cheese inside each cavity and top with spinach and ham strips. Season with salt and pepper and then crack an egg into each. Bake in the oven for 20 minutes on the center rack. Season with salt and pepper, replace the tops, and serve as an all-in-one breakfast.

FIG & BALSAMIC TARTE TATIN

SERVES 4

INGREDIENTS

1/4 cup (60 ml) balsamic vinegar
1/4 cup (60 ml) sugar
9 medium fresh, ripe Black Mission figs, halved
1/2 package (1 sheet) store-bought puff pastry

PREPARATION

Preheat oven to 400°F (200°C). Line the bottom of a 10-inch pie pan with a circle of parchment paper.

In a small pot, bring balsamic vinegar and sugar to a boil and let reduce over low heat for 3 to 4 minutes, until it turns into a syrup. Pour syrup into pie pan and quickly spread over the parchment paper before it sets. Arrange sliced figs, skin sides down, over syrup.

On a lightly floured, flat work surface, roll out dough to about 1/8 inch thick and cut out a circle, about 1-1/2 inches larger than the diameter of the pie pan. Slide pastry over figs, tucking the edges down inside the pan. Pierce with a fork to allow steam to escape. Bake for 30 minutes.

After 30 minutes, carefully turn out tart onto a plate larger than the pie pan. Let sit for 10 minutes before serving.

FRENCH-STYLE FRITTATA

SERVES 6

INGREDIENTS

1 tbsp olive oil
1 cup (250 ml) thick-cut bacon, diced
4 cups leeks, thinly sliced
6 slices raclette cheese, cut in half
6 eggs
1/2 cup (125 ml) milk
2 tbsp flour
Salt and freshly ground pepper

PREPARATION

In a pan, heat olive oil and sauté bacon for 3 to 4 minutes. Add leeks and continue cooking for 2 to 3 minutes. Grease a baking dish and spread half of the bacon and leek mixture at the bottom. Top with half of the cheese and remaining bacon and leek mixture.

Preheat oven to 350°F (175°C).

In a bowl, whisk together eggs and milk. Gradually sprinkle in flour, whisking constantly to prevent lumps from forming. Season with salt and pepper and pour evenly over leeks, bacon, and cheese. Top with remaining cheese slices, and bake for 30 minutes. Serve.

THE ROYAL SCONES

MAKES 16 SCONES

INGREDIENTS

1 cup (250 ml) golden raisins
5 cups flour
2 tbsp baking powder
3/4 cup (180 ml) sugar
Zest of 1 lemon
1 tsp salt
1 cup (250 ml) cold unsalted butter, diced
1-1/2 cups (375 ml) buttermilk
Milk
Sugar

PREPARATION

Soak raisins for 5 minutes in hot water to soften them. Drain well and set aside.

In a bowl, combine flour, baking powder, lemon zest, and salt. Add butter and, using your hands, mix the dough until it has the texture of coarse crumbs. Add buttermilk and raisins and mix until just combined; don't overmix.

Transfer dough to a lightly floured, flat work surface, and roll into a cylinder, about 3 inches in diameter. Chill for 30 minutes. Using a sharp knife, slice into round scones. Transfer to a baking sheet lined with parchment paper, or a silicone baking mat, and chill for 30 minutes.

Preheat oven to 350°F (175°C).

Brush the top of each scone with a bit of milk, and sprinkle with sugar. Bake for 30 minutes. Serve with jam and crème fraîche.

 DID YOU KNOW?

The first scones were round and flat, about as big as a medium-sized plate, and made with unleavened oats. The round cake, called bannock by the Scottish, was cooked in the oven on a griddle and then sliced into triangles for serving.

INGREDIENTS INDEX

CONVERSION CHART

1 dl	10 cl	100 ml
1 tablespoon		15 ml
1 teaspoon		5 ml
1 oz		30 ml
1 cup		250 ml
4 cups		1 l
1/2 cup		125 ml
1/4 cup		60 ml
1/3 cup		80 ml
1 lb		450 g
2 lbs		900 g
2.2 lbs		1 kg
400°F	200°C	T/7
350°F	175°C	T/6
300°F	150°C	T/5

Volume Conversion
* Approximate values

1 cup (250 ml) crumbled cheese	150 g
1 cup (250 ml) all-purpose flour	115 g
1 cup (250 ml) white sugar	200 g
1 cup (250 ml) brown sugar	220 g
1 cup (250 ml) butter	230 g
1 cup (250 ml) oil	215 g
1 cup (250 ml) canned tomatoes	250 g

NOTES

60

IN THE SAME COLLECTION

THE WORLD'S 60 BEST
SALADS
PERIOD.

THE WORLD'S 60 BEST
PASTA SAUCES
PERIOD.

THE WORLD'S 60 BEST
BURGERS
PERIOD.

THE WORLD'S 60 BEST
LUNCHES
PERIOD.

THE WORLD'S 60 BEST
...ECIPES FOR STUDENTS
PERIOD.

THE WORLD'S 60 BEST
PIZZAS
PERIOD.

THE WORLD'S 60 BEST
GRATINS
PERIOD.

THE WORLD'S 60 BEST
STUFFED DISHES
PERIOD.